How to survive
UNIVERSITY

Clive Whichelow & Mike Haskins

Illustrations by Kate Rochester

summersdale

HOW TO SURVIVE UNIVERSITY

Summersdale Publishers Ltd
46 West Street
Chichester
West Sussex
PO19 1RP
UK

www.summersdale.com

Printed and bound in China

ISBN: 978-1-84953-139-9

Substantial discounts on bulk quantities of Summersdale books are available to corporations, professional associations and other organisations. For details contact Summersdale Publishers by telephone: +44 (0) 1243 771107, fax: +44 (0) 1243 786300 or email: nicky@summersdale.com.

To...

From...

Other titles in this series:

INTRODUCTION

The life of an undergrad looks so inviting — living away from home, cheap drinks, freedom and no parents to interfere. But on the other hand you've got to pay for everything yourself and there is no one to do your cooking, washing, ironing and cleaning!

So this little book is here to help you survive the ups and downs, the ins and outs, the dos and don'ts and probably the shoulds and shouldn'ts of university life.

Without it, how would you know how to provide a nutritious meal for one on 49p, how to wear the same T-shirt for a fortnight without anyone noticing or how to get drinks bought for you all night without being labelled a tightwad?

Plus, you'll have to learn how to shrug off accusations of being a useless sponging layabout. In 20 years' time your generation will be running the country so why shouldn't you let off a bit of steam now? The old gits of this world are just jealous. Enjoy!

THINK POSITIVELY

Don't fret about leaving home; your
parents will suddenly appreciate you
more than ever!

Don't worry about the disgusting food
and living conditions; just think how
strong your immune system will be by the
end of it all

Don't think of it as a student loan; think of it as the government's round (every night for three years)

REALITY CHECK

You do have to attend lectures occasionally (thank goodness your mobile phone has a weekly alarm setting)

Instead of sharing a house with tidy, clean parents you may now be sharing with someone who has an even greater disregard for hygiene than you do

You will have to be careful with your money — though whether you're quite so careful with everyone else's (your parents', the government's, etc.) is another matter entirely

Re-sits are even less fun than normal exams, so try to get through on the first attempt

EMBRACE STUDENT LIFE WITH A GOOD DOSE OF IRONY

Wear sackcloth and ashes and plead poverty (especially when speaking to parents)

Apply to do a three-year scientific study of indolence among university students and at the end hand in a completely blank dissertation

On your graduation portrait, have yourself photographed with a large dollop of wet cement and a trowel balanced on top of your mortar board

THINGS IT'S BEST NOT TO CONTEMPLATE

Your student loan will have to be
paid back

Your degree may not be enough to secure
you a job as a burger flipper

After university, you will be invited to fewer toga parties

GOOD AND BAD
ROLE MODELS

Good	Bad
The student who goes down in university history	The student who goes down in history because they got the lowest exam result since records began
The model student	The student who moonlights as a topless model
The student who ends up with several degrees	The student who devotes his time to anything several degrees proof
The student who always gives 100 per cent	The student who always gets 100 per cent – by cheating

SELF-HELP BOOKS YOU MIGHT WANT TO READ

Utter Tripe: 1001 Recipes for Tripe

How to Pad Out Three Facts into a Ten-Page Essay: The Beginner's Guide (by the authors of *How to Pad Out Five Facts into an Entire Degree*)

Think Yourself Brighter

Sure-fire Ways to Convince Your Parents
That You Need More Money

IRRITATING THINGS OTHER PEOPLE WILL START SAYING AND DOING TO YOU

Asking you awkward detailed questions about the subject you're supposed to be studying

Adding the phrase 'at the taxpayers' expense' every time they refer to anything you've been doing while at university

Buying you book tokens instead of proper birthday and Christmas presents

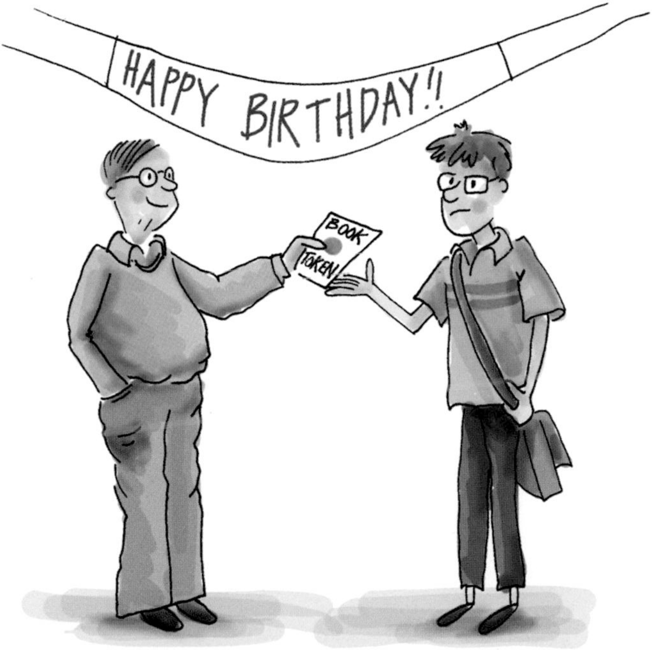
HAPPY BIRTHDAY!!
BOOK
TOKEN

ARGUMENTS YOU MAY FIND YOURSELF FALLING INTO

'Actually Media Studies is a really important course...'

'I'm telling you, someone in this house has opened my strawberry yogurt, eaten some of it and then glued the top back down so I wouldn't notice...'

'But I did the dishes last month...'

'I have to read comics for my dissertation'

'I will pay you back next week, honest'

'I'm not lazy, I'm pacing myself — it's a
three-year course, you know'

TRICKS OF THE TRADE

Wear black — you can wear the same T-shirt for a fortnight without anyone noticing (do remember the deodorant, though)

Bulk-buy eggs and potatoes — the humble potato can be chips, mash or jacket; the egg can be fried, boiled or poached; bread can be toast, sandwiches or pudding... for less than 50p you will have a varied menu every night!

Act with confidence – everyone is panicking when they begin university, so if you can look slightly less terrified than everyone else you will be a king or queen among your fellow students!

Become really good at pool and table football — it will save a fortune when you play 'loser buys the drinks'!

Don't tell everyone you meet what A level results you got — this will make you look slightly more mature than other students

TYPES OF STUDENT YOU COULD BE

Beyond cool — who effortlessly gets top marks all the time without apparently doing any studying whatsoever. (Oh, how they'll all hate you!)

The low achiever — who quickly works out the absolute minimum you can get away with doing to avoid being thrown out

The happy camper — who is endlessly jolly and enthusiastic and first in line to buy a university scarf and sweatshirt from the union shop

COLLEGE SCARVES SOCKS CAPS ETC.

STUDENT UNION

Uni

Uni

Speccy swot – who shuns all parties, gigs and drinking sessions and is often the only person attending a lecture (and that includes the lecturer!)

Even speccier swot – who spends so much time studying that not a single one of their contemporaries will ever remember them being at college

THINGS TO LOOK FORWARD TO AT THE END OF IT

You'll have money to burn (hell, you may even have a job!)

You won't have to subsist on a continuous diet of spag bol and cheap cider

You can go back and live in luxury with Mum and Dad for a while!

When you graduate you will have letters after your name – make sure everyone uses these every time they refer to you for the rest of your life!

SCIENCE AND NON-SCIENCE

Scientists have concluded that an important learning skill is 'episodic memory' — though this doesn't mean being able to recall the plotlines of *EastEnders*

Your brain stops growing when you are aged 18 — but for some reason that's exactly when they pack you off to university

It is a myth that people only use 10 per cent of their brains — this may have come from observing students who manage to study while listening to an iPod, watching TV and eating

HOW TO MAINTAIN ENTHUSIASM

Surely you'll come up with one world-shattering idea during your time at university — even if it's just a fantastic new sort of sandwich filling

See it not as work, but more work avoidance

Tell yourself that one day you will eat food that is not out of a tin or freeze-dried

You spend three years drinking, having sex and getting up late and you're asking for ways to maintain enthusiasm?!

BASIC LESSONS
TO REMEMBER

Some of your fellow students will
eventually become very rich and
successful — so remember to keep any
incriminating photos of them that
you take

Don't make enemies — one of these people may end up being your boss!

Study hard and you could end up being a lecturer and stay at uni forever!

If you think uni's tough, wait till you start working for a living

When writing an essay include detailed quotes from articles written by your tutor — they will be so flattered it will be worth several extra marks

DOS AND DON'TS

Do try to sleep well
Don't do it during lectures

Do remember to phone your
parents occasionally
Don't only do it when you've run out
of money

Do try to eat properly
Don't consider your five a day to include
wine (fruit) or tobacco (leafy vegetables)

FIRST DAY DISASTERS
TO AVOID

Turning up at the wrong university (one of the hazards of letting your dad drive you there)

Discovering that your student flat is a two-hour bus ride from your college

Finding that your tiny new room will not accommodate your entire lifelong stash of possessions from home

Cadging a fag off the principal

Discovering that, owing to an error while
setting up your laptop, you have just
spent your entire student loan on
cheese spread

INADVISABLE SHORTCUTS

Trying to cram all your work into the first six months so you can relax for the rest of the time

Calling your parents hundreds of times in the first week so you won't have to do it for the rest of your course

Booking your place on *University Challenge* before you've had a chance to learn anything

FACTS AND FIGURES

It was Matthew Arnold who described Oxford as the 'city of dreaming spires'

So even in the nineteenth century students were legendary for spending most of their time asleep

A survey showed 10 per cent of recent students were doing nothing whatsoever six months after graduation

Either because of problems in the jobs market or because the students hadn't realised they had graduated due to the terrible hangovers they were still suffering

The first university in Europe to grant degrees was the University of Bologna in 1088. In commemoration of this fact spaghetti Bolognese is regularly eaten by students to this day

FANTASIES YOU MAY START HAVING

The student loan company sends you a letter telling you not to worry about paying the money back

You discover that, to your complete surprise, you have completed your overdue dissertation last night while blind drunk, and it's a work of genius!

A famous film director wants to cast you in the starring role of the British remake of *Animal House*

You are back at primary school where a 50-word essay on 'What I Did On My Holidays' brings you plaudits and acclamations from staff and parents alike

You are in fact studying for a Masters degree in mastery of games for Xbox

READY RESPONSES FOR THINGS OTHERS WILL SAY TO YOU

'Do you realise I'm paying for you to be at university?!'

'Great! I'll send the bill right over!'

'All you do at university is spend three years lazing around, drinking and having sex!'

'Yes. I was lucky to get on that course'

'Are you going to be able to get any sort
of job once you've got your degree?'
'Yes. I've applied to be head of hiring and
firing at your firm'

'Lucky you – all those long holidays...'
'If you call six weeks fruit picking for
peanuts a holiday'

REALISTIC AND UNREALISTIC GOALS IN YOUR NEW LIFE

Realistic: Leaving university with lots of
happy memories
Unrealistic: Leaving university with
a fortune amassed from your newly
invented social networking website

Realistic: Making new friends and having lots of fun

Unrealistic: Meeting an heir to a fortune who whisks you away to a life of luxury in some tropical paradise

Realistic: Getting a good mark for your first essay

Unrealistic: Your first essay is so good that the university immediately renames the lecture hall in your honour

THINGS YOU'LL FIND YOURSELF WORRYING ABOUT

Unimportant	Important
That you haven't made any friends on your first day	That you haven't made any friends by the end of the three years
That you eat soup made from leftovers	That you don't have leftovers because you haven't eaten for three weeks
You've fallen in love with your lecturer	Your lecturer has taken out a restraining order against you
You're not sure you fully understand certain aspects of your studies	You realise you've just spent three years attending lectures for the wrong course

CHANGES THAT WILL HAPPEN TO YOUR APPEARANCE

You will spend at least some of your time at university wearing a traffic cone on your head

You will take on a grey pallor — from spending three years in a flat with either no windows or extremely dirty ones

You will develop one more muscular arm — due to regular drink lifting

IMPORTANT THINGS
TO REMEMBER

What course you're meant to be doing

It's best to show up to the occasional lecture so everyone doesn't think you've taken a year out

All those drunken layabouts you encounter day to day are the leaders of tomorrow — scary isn't it?

If you weren't suffering a little bit it probably wouldn't all be worthwhile

DRESS TO IMPRESS

With charity shop chic you're beyond fashion (Doc Martens and a tutu with a trilby? Fabulous! Even if you are a bloke)

'Bed-head' is a hairstyle you can proudly sport all year round

Fake tattoos were invented for scaring the life out of your parents at the end of term

WHAT TO DO IF IT ALL GETS TOO MUCH

Ask if you can start all over again — perhaps from year one of primary school onwards

Skip a couple of lectures and chill for a bit — what do you mean, you're already doing that?!

Pamper yourself — have *two* pieces of
toast with your beans

Go for a long drive — assuming you can
get someone to lend you a car, of course

MAKE SOME POSITIVE RESOLUTIONS

I will only skip lectures in extreme
circumstances (e.g. oversleeping,
hangover, forgetting what day
it is, whatever...)

I will try to make my entire student loan
last at least the first two weeks

I will keep my flat nice and neat and clean
(by spending all my time in someone
else's flat)

REMEMBER – THIS ISN'T A TRIAL RUN!

Your mum and dad are not going to move into your student flat with you (unless they've decided to enrol as mature students and not told you)

On the other hand you could always change course – perhaps it is a trial run after all!

If you don't do the dishes yourself, they'll still be dirty in the morning

DON'T TRY TO LIVE UP TO AN IMPOSSIBLE IDEAL

Despite what other students may tell you, it is inadvisable to do no work at all for three years and just do a couple of days' cramming before the exams

There are no real winners in an 'eating stuff found down the back of the fridge' competition

Britain's university system goes back 800 years, so it may not be easy to be the best student ever

Chariots of Fire was a film, set in 1924 — your university experience may not be identical

DO SOMETHING STUDENTS AREN'T SUPPOSED TO DO

Invest your loan in shares and live off the dividends

Arrive at your parents' home without a
bag containing ten weeks' worth
of laundry

Work!

Leave a party while it's still dark

Drink mineral water and go to bed
early occasionally

THE GOOD NEWS

The good stuff will be great and the bad stuff will provide you with a fund of dinner party stories for the rest of your life

When you finish you should have another qualification to go with your ASBO

The number of students getting first class honours degrees has been steadily rising, so by the time you graduate it'll be virtually guaranteed!

You will be mixing with some of the finest minds of your generation — and may even be beating some of them at *Mario Kart*

It may be hard to believe sometimes when you look around at your mates, but you guys are this country's elite!

www.summersdale.com